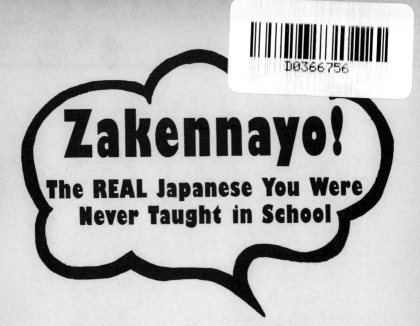

Zakennayo!

The REAL Japanese You Were Never Taught in School

Philip J. Cunningham

Illustrated by Kim Wilson Brandt

A PLUME BOOK

PLUME
Published by the Penguin Group
Penguin Books USA Inc., 375 Hudson Street,
New York, New York 10014, U.S.A.
Penguin Books Ltd, 27 Wrights Lane,
London W8 5TZ, England
Penguin Books Australia Ltd, Ringwood,
Victoria, Australia
Penguin Books Canada Ltd, 10 Alcorn Avenue,
Toronto, Ontario, Canada M4V 3B2
Penguin Books (N.Z.) Ltd, 182–190 Wairau Road,
Auckland 10, New Zealand

Penguin Books Ltd, Registered Offices:
Harmondsworth, Middlesex, England

First published by Plume, an imprint of Dutton Signet,
a division of Penguin Books USA Inc.

First Printing, November, 1995
10 9 8 7 6 5 4 3 2

℗ REGISTERED TRADEMARK—MARCA REGISTRADA

LIBRARY OF CONGRESS CATALOGING-IN-PUBLICATION DATA:

Cunningham, Philip J.
    Zakennayo! : the real Japanese you were never taught in school / Philip J. Cunningham ;
illustrated by Kim Wilson Eversz.
        p.   cm.
    ISBN 0-452-27506-7
    1. Japanese language—Slang. 2. Japanese language—Obscene words. 3. Japanese
language—Conversation and phrase books—English. I. Eversz, Kim Wilson. II. Title.
PL696.C86   1995
495.6'7—dc20
                                                                                    95-154
                                                                                    CIP

Printed in the United States of America
Set in Janson
Designed by Leonard Telesca

BOOKS ARE AVAILABLE AT QUANTITY DISCOUNTS WHEN USED TO PROMOTE
PRODUCTS OR SERVICES. FOR INFORMATION PLEASE WRITE TO PREMIUM
MARKETING DIVISION, PENGUIN BOOKS USA INC., 375 HUDSON STREET, NEW
YORK, NEW YORK 10014.

FROM THE LAND OF THE RISING SUN—
REAL JAPANESE EXPRESSIONS

O-CHA SHINAI?
Will you not have some tea?
(the standard pickup line used on the street)

OTOTOI KOI!
Bug off!
(literally, "Disappear yesterday!")

BAKA!
Stupid!

KENKA UTEN NOKA?
You lookin' for a fight?

KUCHI NI CHAKKU!
Shut up!

YOAKE NO HOHI ISSHO NI SHITAI.
Let's have morning coffee.
(subtle way of saying "Let's spend the night together.")

IERO KYABU.
Easy woman.
(literally, "Yellow cab," a name inspired by the
observation that New York cabs are "easy to pick up")

HYAKU NIN GIR.
Man of a hundred conquests.

Special thanks to all the people who taught me Japanese slang whether they knew it or not.

Contents

Contents

Contents

Foreword

Zakennayo! picks up on Japanese where the dictionary leaves off. Japanese say *"Zakennayo!"* when they're angry, frustrated, and mad. They shout it, mumble it, and mutter it in situations they don't like. The French say *"Merde!"*, the Spanish say *"¡Mierda!"*, the Italians say *"Merda!"*, and the Japanese say, well, *"Zakennayo!"* This word has a real zing to it, especially on the crowded streets of Japan. It means "Don't fuck with me!" and disproves the myth that the Japanese are always polite.

Zakennayo! If you are in Japan watching an American movie with Japanese subtitles, you may be surprised to see that "fuck you," "asshole," "bug off," and "cut the shit" are all expressed with just one word—*zakennayo!* It's rude, yet it conveys the point with just a touch of restraint, and is originally based on the term *"fuza-keru na,"* which means "to romp around"—"not." It's a way of getting people to give you a wide berth; it announces that you are a contender.

This guide to Japanese slang takes you out of the classroom and puts you on the mean streets of Tokyo to sink or swim. An American character named Kenny will help you navigate the back alleys and taboo regions of Tokyo with mischievous humor and devilish delight.

Each chapter focuses on one part of town with a look at one particular subculture. Dialogues in romanized Japanese are followed by English translations and vocabulary lists.

Introduction: Foreign Affairs

If you're reading this book, chances are you're a *gaijin*. Welcome to the club. You are now a member of one of the diverse ethnic groups in the world, an identity you share with the entire world population minus the Japanese.

Welcome to Japan, *gaijin*. Here in the land of the rising sun, you are a member of a troublesome minority. You are the eternal outsider.

The good news, *gaijin*, is that you will get extra attention. The bad news is that much of it will not be to your advantage. *Gaijin* find it difficult to rent an apartment, obtain a non-English teaching job, or marry the girl next door. *Gaijin* are a cross between the ignorant barbarian and the dreamy Hollywood star.

Gaijin of the world, you're different. So accept the fact that:

1. You will never fit in.
2. You probably don't want to fit in.

3. The more you understand, the more paranoid you will get.
4. When you are linguistically insulted, excluded, mocked, and ignored by the fluent Japanese speakers around you, there's no better way to get even than by dropping the mot juste in their exclusive language. Try this for a start. Put the accent on the second syllable, *zaKENnayo!* Say it loud. Make it sing. For more vocabulary, read chapters 3 through 12.
5. Your Japanese will never be as effective as your English, even if your English isn't that good, so pepper your Japanese with lots of English.

Despite the desire to remain culturally elusive, most Japanese are hospitable, well-mannered, and patient to a fault, so you'll probably have a great time.

Gaijin are outnumbered by a factor of ten thousand to one. Everything you do and say is magnified by your appearance. Most times it's better to be quiet and inscrutable, but know when to flip 'em the bird, linguistically speaking. Use your slang with care with strangers, but let it rip with friends who will be shocked, surprised, and break into giggles. *ZaKENnayo!* How did you know that?

I
Alien Invaders

Gaijin da! (It's a foreigner!)

Let's follow Kenny around Tokyo and see if we can't master some slang along the way. Tokyo is the inspiration for all cities in today's Japan, so its distinct neighborhoods boast national importance. Kenny and his friends will take us on a sociolinguistic tour of some of the more questionable parts of town.

Kenny is an American English teacher, Nigel is a British newswriter, and Sharon is an Australian hostess. In Japan they are the same species, simply *gaijin*. Taro, a Japanese-American from Hawaii, is as American as Kenny, but he doesn't look like the others, so he is never called *gaijin*. Keiko is "pure" Japanese, so she has trouble understanding why foreigners don't like being called *gaijin*.

Nigel works for a conservative Japanese television station. He is formal and a bit uptight as reflected in his textbook Japanese. On the other hand, Kenny, the lazy English teacher, is so good at street slang he's beginning to sound downright sleazy.

Ne'er-do-well Taro has an awesome slang vocabulary. Keiko, who likes to hang out with foreigners, tends to be formal in speech because she comes from a very rich family. Sharon has been in Japan so long she'd rather speak English, but her Japanese is right on and totally uninhibited. Watch how they interact and decide who you'd rather be.

After a few years in Japan, Kenny and Nigel have become tired of hearing the word *gaijin*, even though it simply means outsider. They've done a little homework to see if they can find a better way of saying foreigner. Here are some of the alternatives, most of which make them wish they were simply called *gaijin* again.

Talking About Gaijin

Here's a conversation Kenny and Nigel overheard on the pedestrian bridge by Harajuku station at lunchtime. Two slutty school dropouts with thick makeup and permed hair are looking over the two foreign men. The *para gal* (young disco dancer) is talking to her friend, *ike-ike gal* (slightly less young disco type).

PARA GAL: **Ano hito wa hafu mitai.**

NIGEL: What did she say, Kenny?

KENNY: She said **ano hito,** meaning that person, looks like a **hafu,** which means half-breed. She must be talking about you, Nigel, with your dark James Bond looks!

NIGEL: Shh!, wait, now what is she saying?

PARA GAL: **Aitsu wa inchiki gaijin.**

KENNY: She said **aitsu,** meaning that creep, looks like **inchiki gaijin,** which means a "wannabe" foreigner.

NIGEL: Well, Kenny, and who do you suppose she's talking about now?

IKE-IKE GAL: **Jingai bakari.**

KENNY: Hear that? She said **jingai,** that's **gaijin** backward! **Jingai bakari** means nothing but foreigners.

PARA GAL: **Takenoko ga dan dan inakunatchatta.**

NIGEL: Now what is she saying?

KENNY: She said the **takenoko,** which means local punks, are **dan dan** (gradually) **inakunatchatta** (disappearing).

PARA GAL: **Takoku-sekigun mitai.**

KENNY: She said we look like multinational forces. Hey, Nigel, let's forget this cheap trim, I'm in the mood for some real **sushi.** I just love **maguro.**

NIGEL: Isn't there a sushi shop just around the corner?

KENNY: Not that kind, stupid. I'm talking about pussy.

Dialogue in English

PARA GAL: Look at that one, I think he's a half. The other creep looks like a cheap foreigner.

IKE-IKE GAL: So many wetbacks.

PARA GAL: There are fewer "bamboo shoots" these days. It's like packed with the multinational forces.

Vocabulary

ano hito   that person

17

hafu	half-breed
aitsu	that creep; can be friendly or not, depending on circumstances
bakari	nothing but
jingai	*gaijin* with syllables reversed; cool, plus foreigners don't understand it.
inchiki gaijin	bogus foreigners, cheap foreigners; usually used to refer to "semi" Caucasians, often a reference to workers of Mideastern origin
takenoko	"bamboo shoots"; young Japanese punks who hang out by Yoyogi park in Tokyo
takoku-sekigun	a word that became popular during the Gulf War and subsequent UN actions involving international forces; for Japanese kids unfamiliar with war and foreigners, *takoku-sekigun* sums up the exotics in their midst

More Vocabulary

To the appearance-conscious Japanese, what better way is there to judge foreigners than superficially? Asians tend to be viewed by nationality; people of European and African descent are judged by color.

paki

firipina

japayuki

Pakistani; a dark-skinned man, could be Indian or Sri Lankan
Filipina; a Southeast Asian woman; dark-skinned Japanese
Jap-asian; a Filipina or other Asian who acts and dresses Japanese, usually in the sex business

banchopari	half-Korean, half-Japanese
chugokujin	Chinese, who, thanks to a glorious history, are viewed as the highest status Asians outside of Japan, which is, of course, considered number one
tai jin	Thais
indo jin	Indian; anyone who looks vaguely south Asian
arabu jin	Arabs
yudaya jin	Jews
isuraeru jin	Israelis
iran jin	Iranians
nisei	second-generation Japanese descent
sansei	third-generation Japanese descent
nikei burajiru jin	Brazilians of Japanese descent
chosen jin	Korean (considered impolite); usually refers to Japanese residents of Korean descent associated with North Korea
kankoku jin	Korean; also refers to Japanese-born Koreans associated with South Korea
haku jin	a white, Caucasian
koku jin	a black person
dojin	earth person, used in reference to blacks
ameko	American, Yank
itako	Italian, wop
kimpatsu	blond
patsukin	blonde
akage	redhead, carrot top

kurombo	black, darkie
kusekke	wavy-hair types
i jin	a general way to say foreigner or alien
gaigokujin	outside country person; considered more polite, but the meaning is about the same, like saying foreigner instead of alien
gaijin-sama	is structurally polite, but the nuance of meaning still depends on the goodwill of the speaker. For example, *chotto gaijin-sama dame* literally means "we don't take honorable foreigners," but actually it is an outright rejection based on nationality that is more akin to this: "None of them fuckin' so-called honorable foreign barbarians are allowed into my pure Japanese-only establishment. Take a walk!"
ainoko	"a love child," a half-Japanese child. This seemingly innocuous word, often used to refer to a child of African American–Japanese heritage, was edited out of the film *Rising Sun* when it was shown in Japan.

hafu
"a half," a kid of mixed blood, as in half-Japanese, half–something else. An African-American filmmaker is trying to get these kids renamed doubles for their rich dual culture.

daburu
"a double," a child of mixed parentage

The discrimination applied to foreigners has deep roots in domestic discrimination among Japanese. Japanese who are different by birth are called:

burakumin
Japanese outcasts (taboo word) traditionally engaged in "lower-caste" trades such as leather tanning and the meat business

eta
another way of saying *burakumin*; both of these terms make liberal-minded Japanese listeners squirm

ainu
the original inhabitants of the islands, aborigines

kansai jin
Japanese from western Japan, Osaka area

edokko
Japanese from Tokyo

Japanese who are different by choice are called:

chapatsu
tea-colored hair (bleached or dyed hair)

ki-irogami	refers to yellow-haired kids, usually teenage rebels who bleach their hair blond
gaisen	a Japanese girl who only dates *gaijin*
hama o	"a hammer boy" (as in MC Hammer); a Japanese boy who dresses and acts "black" to attract *hama ko*
hama ko	"a hammer girl"; Japanese girl who likes street fashion and dating black men
bobbi-o	same as *hama o*, inspired by Bobby Brown
bobbi-ko	same as *hama ko*, inspired by Bobby Brown
marukomu ekksu	Malcolm X; followers of black fashion, like those who wear one of Spike Lee's widely marketed "X" caps

Aware of how "sensitive" foreigners can be, Japanese have a polite generic way of referring to the strangers in their midst: **ano hito** means that person, and it can almost be considered a compliment since the fact that you are a human being is not questioned. It's used to refer obliquely to a *gaijin* in a crowded situation.

Facts of Life for English Teachers

Kenny says all foreigners in Japan are English teachers.
"But I'm not an English teacher," Nigel protests. "I work at a TV station."

"Wrong!" shouts Kenny. "All *gaijin* are English teachers, like it or not, and you're expected to put out."

So here are a few snappy answers to discourage the free English lessons until you master the contents of this book.

Hello. Can you teach me English?

Boku wa eigo no sensei ja nai.
I am not an English teacher.

This is not very convincing. You might want to try:

Boku wa furansu jin desu.
I am French.

This clever response falls flat on its face, however, if the next line is:

Bonjour. Can you teach me English?

The point is, all *gaijin* are supposed to speak English, so be prepared for a linguistic tug of war.

Since Japanese are known to value conformity you can bank on hearing the same questions over and over.

1. *Shushin wa doko desu ka?*
   Where are you from?
2. *O-ikutsu desu ka?*
   How old are you?
3. *Shumi wa nan desu ka?*
   What are your hobbies?

When you get tired of answering truthfully—as Nigel would—use your imagination. Here's what Kenny would say:

1. **Boku wa kasei kara kimashita.**
   I come from Mars. (Sometimes you'll actually feel that way, too.)
2. **Kimi no taiju wa nan kilo?**
   How much do you weigh? (Answer a question you don't want to answer with a question your questioner does not want to answer. It works wonders.)
3. **Shumi ga nai.**
   I have no hobbies. (This answer, short and sweet, often helps bring an unwanted conversation to a conclusion.)

Finally, watch out for the patronizing compliments that usually mean the opposite of what they say.

Yu supiku Japanezu beri weiru (usually said to you in heavily accented English).
The best answer is to pretend you didn't understand the compliment: "What? What did you say?"

Hashi daijobou?
You can use chopsticks?
Here's your way to bring the "look-the-dog-can-do-math-problems" mutual admiration meeting to a rapid close. Answer in kind.

Fo-ku ga tsukaemasuka?
Do you know how to use a fork?
Jozu desu ne!
That's just brilliant!
Watashi wa _____ desu. (insert nationality)
I am _____.

Remember that the verb goes at the end of the sentence; use *ka* to make it a question.
Anata wa _____ desu *ka*? (insert nationality)
Are you _____?
Use *janai* to deny a statement; e.g., *"Watashi wa America jin ja nai."* I am not American.

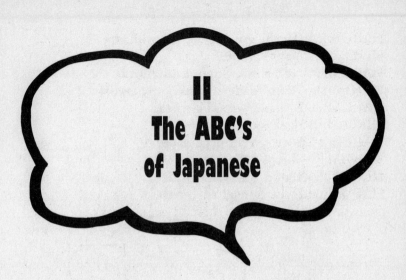

II
The ABC's
of Japanese

Kenny is an English teacher. His students call him *sensei* to his face and *senko* behind his back, which is worse than saying "Hey, Teach!" Kenny works at an all-girls school. He thinks he has a high-status job because everyone is polite to him and compliments him on his English.

He's not complaining. The work is easy, it takes no preparation, and, the way he looks at it, he's getting paid fifty dollars an hour for speaking his native language to cute women.

Right now, Kenny's taking roll call in his last class of the day. While he is going through the ABC's of his attendance book, his chatty students are reviewing their ABC's, too.

While Kenny goes through the forty-odd names on the alphabetical attendance sheet, his "innocent" students, Harumi and Hiromi, are chatting in whispered tones.

Girl Talk

HARUMI: **Kyo wa T-bakku haiterunda.**
HIROMI: **Kino no kare tono deto, dodatta?**

HARUMI: **Bacchi gu. Mecha tanoshikatta.**
HIROMI: **Nani shitano?**
HARUMI: **"H" shita. Sono ato denitta.**
HIROMI: **Doko made itta? A? B? masaka C?**
HARUMI: **B made yo. CIA datta.**
HIROMI: **Fera wa?**
HARUMI: **Sore wa himitsu dayo.**
KENNY: **Shizuka ni shinasai!**
HIROMI: **Senko wa etchi jiji dana.**
HARUMI: **Ii na. Sensei to yaritai.**

Dialogue in English

HARUMI: I'm wearing thong-back panties today.

HIROMI: How did your date go with that guy?

HARUMI: Cool, we really messed around.

HIROMI: What did you do?

HARUMI: We fooled around, then we did a little Denny's action.

HIROMI: How far did you get in your ABC's?

HARUMI: Just a B. We sucked mouth and he played with my tits. I was on the rag.

HIROMI: Did you give him a blow job?

HARUMI: That's for me to know and you to find out.

KENNY: Quiet down, class!

HIROMI: Nice, I want to do it with him.

HARUMI: Teach is a dirty old man.

Teen Talk for the Joys of Sex

Kenny's students, like other high schoolers in Japan, have their own way of learning the alphabet. It starts like this: *A* stands for kiss, *B* is petting, *C* is sex. The first three letters, pursued without caution, lead to *D*, pregnancy. *I* is the unhappy result of actions *A* through *D*, namely abortion.

For this same sexually precocious adolescent crowd, the term *CIA* (pronounced she-eye-ay) is a secret code word. It does not refer to a well-known spy organization, but stands for *Chotto Ima Anne*, which means "Excuse me, but I'm having my period now." Other words for that time of the month include *hatabi* (flag day) or *akabi* (red day).

Perhaps the most euphemistic term of all for "that time of month" is *okyaku san ga kuru*, which means "I have a guest coming." This term is used almost exclusively between women with the result that many men don't "get it." *M*, pronounced *eh-moo*, and *mensu,* short for the English word *men-struation*, are also used.

H is probably the most provocative English letter of all. It means sex, dirty, lascivious. *H-suru,* or "to H" means to do the sex thing. Pronounced *et-chee* in Japanese, this simple English letter manages to be sexy, forbidden, and provocative.

H is also used as an adjective to describe someone who has sex on the mind, as in pervert. *Kare wa H* means "He has sex

on the mind." *H* can also work as a sexual invitation in its verb form, as in *H shitai?* ("Would you like to *H?*"). Why does *H* get all the heat and not *S* or *X* or some other letter? The origin of this word is said to come from the first letter of the romanization of the Japanese reading of the Chinese word for pervert, which is pronounced *hen-tai*.

H is an elegant way to say *pervert*, which gradually expanded in meaning to include normal sex. After all, there is no such thing as proper sex; it is precisely because sex is considered dirty and perverted that makes it so much fun.

What did Harumi and her boyfriend do after sex? *Denitta*. That means they went to Dennys. This particular fast-food restaurant is popular with teenagers because it is ubiquitous, affordable, and allows customers to sit for a long time without being hassled. As a result, Dennys has become a verb. *Deniru?* means "Do you want to do the Dennys thing?" ("Let's go to Dennys.")

Back to the ABC's. *S*, pronounced *eh-su*, is not without sexual connotations, but it usually refers to wad of sperm, as in an oral dose of *bitamin S*, or come. Another hidden meaning of *S* is sister, meaning lesbian. Besides referring to menstruation, *M* can mean masochist, masturbate, or masculine. For the "in" crowd, English abbreviations are easier to say and have a cooler ring, perhaps due to the deliberate ambiguity of many possible meanings.

For some more confusion, a *TV gal* is not a woman you see on television, but a *t*echnical *v*irgin, a young woman who has yet to score a home run. Another term for young people who have yet to do the deed is *mu-jirushi-ryo-hin* or "no-name product," which means they haven't got a name yet.

An *AV gal* in contrast is a woman you see on television, but only if you rent a pornographic video or get the equivalent of the Playboy channel on cable. *AV* suggests audio visual, but actually means adult video. *AV* girls and the dozens of magazines they inspire scream out for your attention in nearly every convenience store and video rental shop in Japan. *AV* sounds like *ebi*, which happens to rhyme with the word for shrimp. Speaking of fish, the vague resemblance that *sushi* and *sashimi* bear to the naked female organ has not gone unnoticed. Watch out for double entendre when talking about *maguro:* (tuna sushi), it means a lousy lay. Take care with *kai* (shellfish), *tako* (octopus), and *hamaguri* (clams). The dirty-minded listener might think you're referring to a woman's pussy.

Fera means fellatio, a blow job. If you're in Japan and you don't want to be understood and you think you're being clever by using "uncommon" English words like *pussy, fuck, 69, fellatio, beaver, clitoris, crevice, crack, box,* and *hole* on a crowded train, think again. All of these words have explicit sexual meaning as loanwords in Japanese. Just as English speakers use a lot of scientific-sounding Latin when talking about sex, Japanese like to use cosmopolitan English.

Speaking of numbers, *69,* when used to refer to mutual oral sex, is not *rokkyu* but *sikkusu nain,* based on the English pronunciation minus the *ty* in sixty-nine.

SF refers not to science fiction, but to a very special kind of relationship. Short for sex friend, an *SF* is someone you can screw around with on a regular basis without commitment.

Ike-ike is Japanese for go-go and refers to young, slightly sluttish girls who like to dress up and go to discos where, if in the right mood, they will get up on the stage and dance in their miniskirts, showing off their *T-bakku* (thong-back) underwear to deliberately provoke the male audience of *jiji* (older men) and *salarimen* (salaried workers).

Discos in the countryside, playing catch-up ball with Tokyo's, are said to feature women wearing ever shorter skirts and *L-bakku* panties, which are half the size of *T*-backs. *O*-backs feature a hole just where you might expect it. The latest rage in regional discos, in Nagoya particularly, is the *no-pan* look. *No* means no, and *pan* sounds like the French word for bread, but in this case it means—you guessed it—no panties! *3P,* pronounced "san pee" means ménage à trois.

WC is a universal term for toilet, but Japanese high schoolers who dream of going to Disneyland give it an American twist: *Wesuto kosuto,* or west coast, means toilet! For the more politically minded youth, *W*ashington *C*lub has the same meaning.

III

Street Jive

Shibuya

Shibuya is a key rail hub that sports a dazzling variety of department stores, restaurants, and bars. Nearby Dogenzaka is home to one of the biggest concentrations of love hotels in Japan. Neighboring Yoyogi Park is jam-packed on Sundays when amateur rock bands line the street. No wonder Kenny and Nigel choose to work in this neighborhood.

Shibuya has an extremely youthful image, to the extent that some adults find it almost repulsive. *Shibukajizoku* refers to the teenagers who hang out on the streets of Shibuya, one of Tokyo's fashionable shopping districts. *Shibu* (Shibuya) *kaji* (short for *kajuaru*, which comes from the word *casual*), and *zoku*, which means tribe. Put it all together and what have you got? Spoiled, rootless, alienated youth.

The so-called *chima* (from the English word *team*) are Tokyo's newest urban youth tribe, the scruffy high school kids who can't afford or don't want to spend money in Shibuya's expensive restaurants and bars and end up hanging out and getting drunk on the street at all hours, often till sunrise.

Bucchigiru means to escape from class. A variation of the word *sabotage*, *saboru* in Japanese, is also used as slang for cutting classes. *Yori michi*, a rather limp excuse for not making it to class, means kicking the dust or traipsing the pavement.

Unfortunately, the street where *chima* hang out, called *senta gai* (Central Street), is now a nest of crime, especially in the environs of the noisy, crowded *gei sen* or game centers. The well-tanned, sloppily dressed characters you might see include *yanki* (fake Yankees), *kiroi kami* (bleached-hair crowd), *oka safa* (surfers in appearance only, hillbilly-surfer boys), and *DJ* types. If the trend of violent crime continues, the word *oshare* (fashionable) will no longer be used to describe Shibuya, and the word *anzen* (safe) will no longer be synonymous with Tokyo.

Kiddy City

Kenny and Nigel have plans to meet Taro, Sharon, and Keiko in Shibuya, after which they will go out for dinner, a drink, and maybe some dancing. Taro has his own ideas. Nigel has asked Keiko out on a date, which leaves Kenny empty-handed. However, if everything goes well, Kenny (the eternal optimist) won't be going home to an empty bed tonight.

Nigel and Kenny meet after work and take a stroll down Senta-gai in Shibuya, heading for the station.

NIGEL: I'm a little nervous about meeting Keiko-san today. I think she's mad at me.

KENNY: What are you wasting your time with an **ojosama** like her for? You want action with the local trim? You gotta learn **nanpa**.

NIGEL: Oh, Kenneth, my old mate, you make it sound so
          easy.
KENNY: Here comes an **OL**, let's check her out.

Zakennayo!

KENNY: **Konnichiwa, ima hima?**
GIRL: *(to herself)* **Bikkuri shita.**
KENNY: **Mushi sareta.**

Dialogue in English

KENNY: Do you have some time?
GIRL: I'm shocked (that you, a foreigner, have the nerve to talk to me without a proper introduction).
KENNY: I just got the cold shoulder.

Vocabulary

ojosama	a preppy woman, a spoiled rich girl
nanpa	flirt, pick-up girls, go fishin' in the crowd
OL	(pronounced *o-eru*) an office lady; they all tend to have long hair and wear frumpy dresses
konnichiwa	hello, greetings, good day
ima hima	Are you free now? Do you have some time?
bikkuri shita	I'm shocked, you scared me
mushi sareta	I've been ignored, I got the cold shoulder

Tea Time

Kenny tries a different pickup line with a more hip-looking girl.

KENNY: **Hi! Derumo mitai-na kanojo o-cha shinai?**
OL: **Yoisho shittate dameyo. Mata kondone.**
KENNY: **Ja, renraku saki oshiete kureyo.**
OL: **Nara eigo shabereru-yo ni naritai kara, oshiete-yo.**
KENNY: **Maji ni, kondo, boku no uchi de, puraibeto ressan shiyo-yo.**

Dialogue in English

KENNY: Hey, babe! I bet all the boys love you. How about some tea?
OL: Thanks for the compliment but no way. See you next time.
KENNY: Okay. How can we get in touch?
OL: I hope you can teach me English. I want to be able to speak.
KENNY: No kidding. Tell you what, let's have a private lesson in my room.

Vocabulary

derumo   beautiful; reversal of English *model*

o-cha shinai?   Will you not have some tea?; the standard pickup line used on the street

yoisho-suru	to praise someone (from the sound of a worker's grunt, or hey-ho)
dameyo	no, not possible; for a nation that can't say no, *dame* is about as negative as you can get
mata kondo ne	How about next time?; sometimes a polite brush-off
renraku saki	contact point; a smooth way to ask for a telephone number
oshiete kureyo	teach me, tell me
kureyo	a casual, breezy request
shabereru-yo ni naritai	I want to have the status of being able to speak; an indirect plea that suggests English lessons are desired
maji ni	Really? Do you mean it?
shiyo-yo	let's, as in Let's do it!

Picking Up

NIGEL: Here comes a **yamato nadeshiko**.

KENNY: Get real, she looks more like a **yanki** who just came from an **ikki-ikki** party. Go for it, man.

NIGEL: **Sumimasen. Shibuya-eki wa doko desu ka?**

YANKI GAL: **Gero-gero, gaijin da. Eigo wakanne yo.**

NIGEL: **Watashi wa nihongo o hanashimasu.**

KENNY: **Ore mo nihongo shabereru-yo ere. Omae Nihon-jin daro?**

NIGEL: **Konnichiwa, anata wa totemo kirei desu . . .**

YANKI GAL: **Wakatteru jan.**

Dialogue in English

NIGEL: Excuse me, where is Shibuya Station?
YANKI GAL: Gross out, a foreigner! I don't know English.
NIGEL: I am speaking in Japanese.
KENNY: I can rap in Japanese, too. Are you Japanese, or what?
NIGEL: Hello, you are beautiful.
YANKI GAL: You finally figured it out.

Vocabulary

yamato nadeshiko	a classical, original Japanese girl, innocent
yanki	Yankee, fake American, Japanese punks who often dye or bleach hair for red and blond tints
ikki–ikki	chug party, shots of liquor
eki wa doko desu ka?	Where is the train station?; the technique of making believe you are lost as a bid for conversation has more credibility when used by foreigners
gero-gero gaijin	Gross out, foreigners!
ore-omae	I–you, in the low-status variation; use only with close friends and serious enemies.

Putting Down

A tough-looking **chima** *comes over to check out the scene.*

CHIMA: **Nani ittenda teme? Kenka utten noka?**
KENNY: **Omae wa dare da? baka ka?**
CHIMA: **Kono yaro. Zakennayo! Ototoi koi!**

Kenny signals to Nigel it is time to leave.

NIGEL: *(to Chima)* **Sumimasen, osewa ni narimashita.**
CHIMA: **Inpo, yaro-u, atchi ni ikeyo.**
KENNY: **Kuso gaki.**

Dialogue in English

CHIMA: What the fuck are you saying? You looking for a knuckle sandwich?
KENNY: And who the fuck are you? Asshole.
CHIMA: Shithead, Fuckin' A. You better scram.
NIGEL: I'm sorry if we have imposed on you in any way.
CHIMA: You fuckin' limp dick, get out of here.
KENNY: You shit-faced devil, you.

Vocabulary

teme	an even ruder way of saying "you"
kenka uten noka	You lookin' for a fight?
omae wa dare da?	Who the fuck are you?
baka ka?	stupid asshole
kono yaro	you asshole (literally, field man)

zakennayo!	Fuck off!
ototoi koi!	Disappear yesterday!
inpo	impotent, wimp
yaro-u	jerk, asshole
atchi ni ikeyo	get lost, go away
kuso gaki	you shitty little devil

Regrets

The girls watch the two pale foreigners walk off in a huff.

STREET GAL: Ima no ameko hansamu de moteso na kanji, nigashita sakana wa ookikatta kamo ne.

YANKI: Gaijin to yaritai no?

STREET GAL: So yo. Gaijin wa are ga ooki te iu ja nai?

YANKI: Demo, gaijin no chinchin wa funya chin nan datte.

STREET GAL: Demo, braza no musuko wa koka kora no bin mitaitte iu yo.

YANKI: Atashi-wa, hama o no hooga ii.

Dialogue in English

STREET GAL: That Yank was good-looking, the popular type. You sure let a big fish get away.

YANKI: You want to do it with a foreigner?

STREET GAL: Yeah. Haven't you heard? Foreigners have big ones.

YANKI: They might have big dicks, but they're soft dicks from what I hear.

STREET GAL: When it comes to the brothers, the "little boy" is the size of a Coke bottle.

YANKI: Hammer boys are good enough for me.

Vocabulary

ameko	rude way to say "American"
moteso	looks popular, tasty
nigashita sakana ooki	the big fish got away
yaritai	Want to do it? Want to fuck?
are ga ooki	It's big; he has a big dick
chin-chin	dick, pee-pee; childish word for penis
funya chin	limp dick, soft dick
braza	"brother," black, African-American
musuko	"son, little boy"; another way to say dick
koka kora no bin	a Coca-Cola bottle
atashi-wa	as for me (feminine)
hama o	Japanese guy who tries to look and act black like MC Hammer

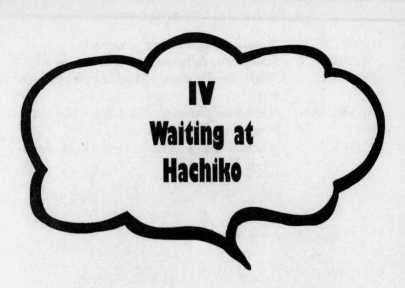

IV
Waiting at Hachiko

Hachiko Statue

Hachiko, the name of a dog enshrined in a bronze statue, is the premier meeting place in Shibuya. If you are waiting for someone who is late or doesn't show, don't feel bad; sooner or later some stranger will come along and make a pass at you.

Getting Picked Up

Sharon has been waiting for ages for Nigel and Kenny to meet her by the famous dog statue Hachiko in front of Shibuya station. She can't help but notice that a smartly dressed, suave-looking Japanese man has been waiting almost as long. She takes off her watch.

SHARON: **Sumimasen, ima nan ji desu ka?**
SALARIMAN: **5:30 desu. Nihongo ga ojozu desu ne.**
SHARON: **Mada mada desu. Machiawase shiteru no?**
SALARIMAN: **Kaisha no doryo to. Machikuta bireta yo. Hachiko ni natta kibun da.**
SHARON: **Watashi mo yo. Akiramete, kohi demo nomi ni ikanai?**

Dialogue in English

SHARON: Excuse me, do you have the time?
SALARIMAN: It's 5:30. Your Japanese is truly excellent.
SHARON: Still learning. Waiting for someone?
SALARIMAN: Yes, a coworker from my company. But I'm sure sick and tired of waiting. It's like I'm turning into a lapdog like Hachiko myself.
SHARON: Me too. If we quit waiting we can go for a coffee or something.

Vocabulary

ima nan ji desu ka?	Do you have the time?; a bid for conversation that establishes this foreigner can speak Japanese
mada mada	still learning

kaisha no doryo to	with my coworker; deemphasizes romantic link
machikuta bireta yo	sick and tired of waiting so long
hachiko ni natta kibunda	I feel like I'm turning into a loyal dog like Hachiko!
akiramete	to give up; enough of this waiting
kohi demo nomi ni ikanai	Let's go for a cup of coffee.

Who's That?

A sharply dressed woman walks up to the man, ignoring Sharon completely. She looks concerned.

WOMAN: **Kono hito dare?**
SALARIMAN: **Osei yo. Mo konakute yokatta noni.**
WOMAN: **Kono gaijin dare?**
SALARIMAN: **Eigo no sensei da yo.**
WOMAN: **Iko yo!**

The man slips his business card to Sharon.

SALARIMAN: **Zettai denwa shite kudasai, mata eigo benkyoshimasho!**

Dialogue in English

WOMAN: And just who is she?
SALARIMAN: You're so late I don't even know why you bothered coming.
WOMAN: Who's the foreigner?
SALARIMAN: Ah, an English teacher.

WOMAN: Well, let's go.
SALARIMAN: Yes, teacher, please call me soon. I want to study more English.

Vocabulary

kono hito dare?	And just who is she?
Eigo no sensei da yo	English teacher; a way to legitimize his contact with foreigner of opposite sex
osei yo	You're so late.
mo konakute yokatta noni	It would have been better if you didn't come at all, why bother?

Being Admired

Sharon is left standing alone as the couple walks off. Her humiliating loss of face did not go unnoticed.

OKA SAFA: **Miro yo! Mabui suke jan?**
DJ: **Suge . . . pai ottsu.**
OKA SAFA: **Ore. Eigo chinpunkanpun, omae shabereyo.**
DJ: **Chotchi wakaru daro. Kanojo karui mitai daze.**
OKA SAFA: **Maji? rakki jan . . . oishi jan . . .**

Sharon waves to Nigel, whose face appears in the crowd.

OKA SAFA: **Yabaiyo kareshi mattetan janai kayo!**
DJ: **Aitsu nanka okama pokku nai ka?**

Zakennayo!

Mild-mannered Nigel sees the boys sitting next to Sharon. He smiles and offers his hand.

NIGEL: **Watashi wa Nai-je-ru desu. Hajimema-shite.**
OKA SAFA: **Uh? I am a pen.**
DJ: **Baka yarou . . .**
NIGEL: **Watashi wa igirisu jin desu.**

The well-tanned street punks give Sharon a lewd lookover as they start to walk away.

DJ: (eyes on Sharon) **Yarite . . .**
SHARON: **Zakennayo!**
DJ: **Cho-yabei, kono suke nihongo wakaru-ze.**

The two punks freeze in astonishment.

NIGEL: Sharon, what did you say to them?
SHARON: Never mind, Mr. Perfect. Let's find the others.

Dialogue in English

OKA SAFA: Hey, check it out! A hot-looking babe.
DJ: With super knockers.
OKA SAFA: It's all Greek to me, but you can rap in English, can't you?
DJ: I can speak English a little. I think she's an easy lay.
OKA SAFA: No shit, lucky us, she looks delicious.

OKA SAFA: Oh fuck, she's waiting for a guy.
DJ: And what a fuckin' fag he is.

51

NIGEL: I am Nigel, pleased to meet you.
OKA SAFA: I am a pen.
DJ: You idiot.
NIGEL: I am English.

DJ: I want to do her.
SHARON: Fuck off!
DJ: Oh, shit, this broad can understand Japanese!

Vocabulary

mabui   cute, pretty; originally Yakuza slang, now popular with youth

suke   Yakuza argot for woman

jan   Is it not? Would you not?; contraction of *ja nai*, which reinforces rather than negates the word it modifies

suge   variation of *sugoi*; wow, cool, far out

pai otsu   tits, comes from reversing syllables of *oppai*, or breast

chinpunkanpun   I have no fuckin' idea about English; it's all Greek to me

shabereyo   speak! sounds cooler than textbook *hanashima-su*

chotchi   a little, just a bit *(chotto)*; also can be used for rejection, as in Just a minute, buddy . . .

maji   really

rakki   lucky

oishi   delicious; this can mean a good setup, a delicious situation in which one stands to reap benefits

yabaiyo	shit, fuck, we blew it
kareshi	boyfriend, main squeeze, "him"
okama poku	looks like a fag, looks queer
I am a pen	Nonsense words of textbook English often come to the fore when a Japanese person gets nervous.
baka	Stupid! You idiot! You fool!; this all-purpose word for *stupid* is written with the characters for horse and deer, stupidly enough
yarite	I want to fuck her.
zakennayo!	Fuck off!
cho-yabe	Damn, we blew it.

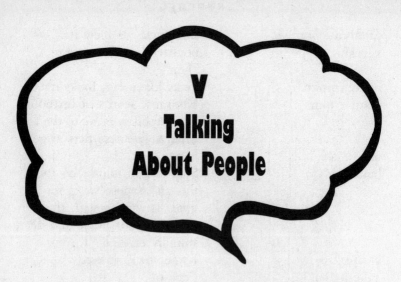

Omotesando Café

The fashion center of Tokyo is a people-watching paradise. Omotesando, located near Meiji Shrine, literally means "outer road leading to the shrine," but today it has a distinct European air. The long boulevard is lined with trees, has wide sidewalks, and is the center of the fashion-and-model industry. Expensive boutiques and street-side cafés make it an excellent location for window-shopping and putting in face time with the beautiful crowd, which includes a healthy dose of foreigners.

Cast of Characters
in a Fashionable Café

moderu	models
iro otoko	hunk, stud
onna tarashi	playboy

otoko tarashi	playgirl
kanojo	girlfriend, main squeeze
kareshi	boyfriend
kizumono	damaged goods, no longer virgin
urenokori	unmarried, hag
kyabasuke	overdressed sluts
obatarian	hen, old auntie
ojamamushi	third-wheel, take a hike (bothersome insect)
putaro	goof-off, bum
ronin	trying to get into school or work
shin jinrui	born after 1965, not hard workers
asobi nin	playboys and playgirls
papa	sugar daddy
dere suke	ladies' man

Waitress Watching

Kenny and Taro sit down in trendy Omotesando café. Waitress Kato-san is bending over in a miniskirt serving drinks.

TARO: Kyo wa mechakomi dane. Keiko to Sharon to Nigel suare-nai na.

KENNY: Konderu hoga mabui suke ni ataru kakuritsu mo takai yo.

TARO: Dasai onna bakari jan ka.

KATO: O-mataseshimashita.

KENNY: Kato Chikako-san, O-hisa desune. Genki?

Kenny just read out loud the Kanji (Chinese ideographs) on her nametag. The waitress stares dumbfounded, ignores Kenny, and walks away.

TARO: **Shikato-sareta.**

KENNY: **Daikon ashi de, decchiri, hana pecha haniwa-gao no kuse ni.**

TARO: **Omae no konomi daro? Pansuto ga dabo dabo no tansoku de, kyabasuke mitai na atsugesho de, suppin o mitara dareka wakannai hodo no nurikabe onna.**

KENNY: **Omae koso anzan gata, chibi, deppa, debu, busu ga suki daro.**

TARO: **Hidee-na.**

Dialogue in English

TARO: Man, this place is packed like sardines. Keiko, Sharon, and Nigel won't have a place to sit.

KENNY: It's better this way, more broads per square foot.

TARO: Yeah, but what if they're all ugly.

KATO: Sorry to keep you waiting!

KENNY: Hey Chikako baby, it's been a while . . . how are you?

TARO: You just got blown off.

KENNY: That's okay, she's just a potato-legged, fat-assed, flat-nosed haniwa.

TARO: Just the way you like it, asshole. Panty hose sliding all over, short legs, sleazy cabaret girl make-up. If you saw her without makeup you wouldn't recognize plaster face.

KENNY: As for you, a-hole, wide hips but short, ugly, and fat with buckteeth, that's your type.

TARO: You're mean.

Vocabulary

mechakomi	crammed, crowded
dasai	ugly, poor
o-hisa	it's been a while (from *hisahiburi*)
shikato suru	to ignore
daikon ashi	potato legs, built like a tank
detchiri	protruding ass
hana pecha	flat-nosed
haniwa-gao	face like a haniwa clay figurine
pansuto	panty hose
dabo dabo	loose and droopy
tansoku	short legs
kyabasuke	sleazy like a cabaret girl
atsugesho	heavy makeup
suppin	no makeup
nurikabe	plaster face
anzan gata	wide hips
chibi	shorty
deppa	buckteeth
debu	fatty
busu	ugly
hidee-na	That's terrible.

Like a Peach

A different waitress walks by.

KENNY: Chotto, kanojo, koko mizu.
KANOJO: Kashikomarimashita.
KENNY: Ano ko hakui na.
TARO: Momo jiri poi kedo, geji mayu dakara inmo ga ko-sou dazo.

KENNY: Ke manju umai-n-dazo. Kuchi ga chisai kara, chitsu mo chisai-n-ja nai ka? Bajin dato omou?

TARO: Ima doki kimusume nanka iru no ka? Oboko ni miete mo dendou kokeshi de, asobi sugi te, taiheiyo de gobou o arau jotai kamo.

KENNY: Keiko to yaritaina.

TARO: Majikayo, ore nara Keiko to neru yori patsu-kin no hoga ii.

Dialogue in English

KENNY: Hey, babe, how about some H$_2$O?

KANOJO: Yes, I understand.

KENNY: She's a real looker.

TARO: Her ass is like a peach, but check out those thick eyebrows—you know she's got pussy hair to match.

KENNY: I love eating pussy. With a small mouth like that you know she's got a tight cunt. You think she's still a virgin?

TARO: You mean there are still virgins these days? Even the ones that look like virgins are probably playing with dildos. You know, if they do it too much, it's like swishing your dick around in the ocean.

KENNY: I'd like to do the deed with Keiko.

TARO: Really? I'd rather do it with a blonde any day.

Vocabulary

koko mizu — How about some H$_2$O?

hakui — beautiful woman

momo jiri	peach ass
geji mayu	thick, dense eyebrows
inmo	secret hair, pubic hair
ke manju	pussy, beaver (hairy bean paste sweet bun)
umai	delicious
chitsu	cunt (technical term)
bajin	virgin
kimusume	virgin
oboko	virgin
dendou kokeshi	dildo
taiheiyo de gobou o arau	"washing a burdock root in the Pacific Ocean"; swishing your dick in a pussy too loose to be desirable

Shut Up!

Keiko, Sharon, and Nigel enter the café.

TARO: **Miro yo, Keiko to Nigel to Sharon ga kita. Uchi ni chaku da!**
NIGEL: **Taro-kun, konnichiwa.**
TARO: **Domo, Sharon, boku no tonari ni dozo.**

Taro motions for Sharon to sit down by him.

SHARON: No thanks. Come on, guys, let's go to Shinjuku for a drink.
KENNY: **Yappa, gaijin-te wagamama dana.**
TARO: **Kedo, Sharon to two shot ni naritai.**

59

Dialogue in English

TARO: Oh, look. Here's Sharon and the others. Better shut your trap.

NIGEL: Hello there, my friend Taro.

Zakennayo!

TARO: Hey, Sharon, aren't you gonna sit next to me?

SHARON: No thanks. Come on, guys, let's go to Shinjuku
           for a drink.

KENNY: Man, those gaijin girls are so full of themselves.

TARO: Yeah, but I want to tango with her.

Vocabulary

kuchi ni chakku   *urusai*, Shut up!

domo   probably the single most
                       versatile word in Japanese;
                       here it means "Hi!" but can
                       also mean "Thank you," "I'm
                       taking leave," etc.

yappa   Of course, see what I mean?

two shot   just the two of them, a couple;
                       pronounced "tsu shotto"

VI
The Gay Life

Ni-Chome

The address known as *Shinjuku Ni-chome* is the center of gay nightlife in Tokyo. A quiet, unassuming neighborhood of small, private bars, it reflects the taboo, near-invisible status of Tokyo's huge gay population. *Ni-chome*, near a small park and the much larger Gyoen Gardens, is on the other side of a busy highway from the crowded, raunchy, heterosexual sex zones of Shinjuku.

Homosexual Slang (pots and pans)

okama	"pot" fag, homosexual man
okama-pokute	wimp, looks faggoty
okama kusai	stinks of being a fag
onnagirai	woman hater, misogynist
rezu kusai	stinks of lesbianism
onabe	"pan," lesbian, homosexual woman

otokogirai	man hater
tachiyaku	the male role (from Kabuki theater in which men play men and men play women)
neko	the female role
shiri o kasu	lend me your ass
ketsu no ana de yaro	do it up the ass
gei	gay, but a homophone of this word also means art, and the overlap between the two has been widely observed; *gei no kai*, meaning "artistic circles," can also be construed as "homosexual circles"

Homosexual Heaven

Sharon, Nigel, Taro, Kenny, and Keiko enter a small bar in the gay mecca of Tokyo.

NIGEL: **Redi fasuto.**
KEIKO: **Hansamu bakari. Onna no ko ni wa tengoku ne.**
KENNY: **Tengoku ja nai, naon wa doko e ichattan da?**
TARO: **Nigel no aite ni do da?**
NIGEL: **Minna-san, biru de ii desu ka?**
MAN: **Oshiri-kashite?**

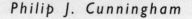

Nigel is at the counter talking to a good-looking man.

TARO: Miro yo, Nigel rakki-jan, aite ga mitsukatta.
KEIKO: Koko tte okama ba nano?
TARO: Nigel wa mecha abunai. Nihongo ga chotto
        o-ne kotoba poishi. Keiko wa zettai anshin.
        Masaka, okoge ja nai daro?
NIGEL: Biru, dozo. Chotto shitsurei, o te arai ni
        ittekimasu.

Zakennayo!

TARO: **Nigel-chan, o toire de ki o tsukete ne, hattenba da yo.**

Dialogue in English

NIGEL: Here we are. Ladies first.
KEIKO: They're all so handsome! A woman's paradise.
KENNY: Not for me. Where'd all the trim go?
TARO: Is Nigel on the prowl?
NIGEL: Can I buy a round of beers for everyone?
MAN: Do you wanna do it with me?

TARO: Look. Isn't Nigel lucky, he found someone!
KEIKO: Is this a gay bar? Abunai!
TARO: It's risky for Nigel, he speaks Japanese like a woman as it is, but you, Keiko, you don't have a thing to worry about. Why, you can be a fag hag.
NIGEL: Excuse me, I'd like to use the men's room.
TARO: Nigel-dear, be careful in the toilet. It's a gay sex bar!

Vocabulary

reidi fasuto	(from English) ladies first
onna no ko ni wa tengoku ne	a woman's paradise
naon	broads, women (*on-na* reversed)
oshiri kashite?	Could you lend me your ass?
okama	gay
mecha abunai	totally dangerous
chotto o-ne kotoba poi	sounds a bit like a fag

65

okoge	women who like to hang out with gay men; "rice that sticks to the pot"
hattenba	public toilet, place for gay sex
neko	the "girl" in a lesbian or homosexual relationship
itachi	the "boy" or bull dyke in a lesbian relationship
neko (yaru)	do the "cat thing," homosexual sex
ura omote	AC/DC, do it both ways, inside and out
kai awase	rubbing pussy
ai name	mutual licking
homo	gay men
rezu	gay women

Lesbians Only

Sharon and Keiko leave for the bar next door, marked "women only," as Nigel returns, buckling his belt.

SHARON: **Keiko-chan, tonari no ba itte mitai? Onna no hito dake haireru no.**

KEIKO: **Iko yo!**

TARO: **Kanojo otoko ni tsumetai, rezu ja nai noka? Dare ga neko de, dare ga itachi da?**

NIGEL: **Ryoho sukebe gyaru sa, ura omote ja nai?**

KENNY: **Nigel shakai no mado ga zenkai dazo.**

NIGEL: **Kanojo-tachi doko e ikimashitaka?**

TARO: Fuck 'em, they want to enjoy **kai awase** and **ai name**.

NIGEL: **Kimi tachi hidoi desu ne. Nihon no homo to**

rezu ga kawai so desu. Jodan ni shinai de
kudasai.

KENNY: Ja, kimi wa kanojo tachi o koko de matte ro,
boku tachi wa sutorippu ba ni iku yo!

Dialogue in English

SHARON: Keiko-chan, you want to take a look at the bar
next door, it's for women only.

KEIKO: Sure, let's go!

TARO: She's cold to men, a lez, right? Who's the cat
and who's the bull dyke?

NIGEL: They're both sex maniacs, probably do it both
ways.

KENNY: Nigel, what do birds do? (Fly—thus, your zip-
per's open.)

NIGEL: And where would the women be now?

TARO: Fuck 'em, they want to enjoy pussy bumping
and cunnilingus.

NIGEL: You guys are so mean. It's bad enough the Japanese force gays in the closet. Do you have to
make fun of them, too?

KENNY: Okay, Taro, Nigel's gonna wait here for the
girls while we take in a strip show!

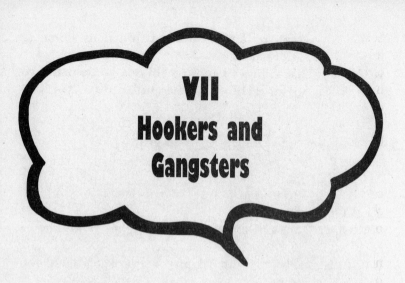

VII
Hookers and Gangsters

Kabuki-Cho

Located on the east side of Shinjuku Eki, the busiest train station in the world, *Kabuki-cho* is teeming with street life and all kinds of vermin, an elaborate Oriental version of Times Square. The strong-arm criminal syndicates that run the sex trade here are no joking matter.

A guide to staying out of trouble in Tokyo's most troubled neighborhood:

1. Don't go there.
2. If you do go there, keep your mouth shut.
3. Make believe you don't speak Japanese if you must talk.
4. If you are about to get in a fight, keep in mind it is more honorable to walk away.

Some of the characters you will see:

yakuza   members of criminal
                          syndicates, Japanese gangsters

baita	whore
joro	slut
chinpira	punks, young yakuza
himo	pimp
dani	a tick, a leech
marubo	a criminal gang
boryoku dan	a violent gang

A slashing motion across the cheek is another way of indicating *yakuza*. A more friendly term is the diminutive *yat-chan*. Punch perm hair, tattoos, and a ducklike gait are typical of *yakuza*.

Recommended fighting words in Japanese, preferably mumbled: *Zakennayo!* But don't say this loud enough for anyone to hear unless you're looking for a fight. You might even be better off saying it in English with a mouthful such as "Fuck you, man! Take a walk! Bug off, buddy! Get lost!"

Cursing in English confuses the listener, which is exactly the point. You get the satisfaction of roundly putting someone down without necessarily having to duke it out. Sometimes that's the best of both worlds. Like the time a combative Japanese guy wanted to fight, and I said, "You'll be sorry." He thought I was apologizing. He only understood the word *sorry*, accepted it as an apology, nodded in recognition, and walked away.

Red Light

Taro and Kenny stand in the doorway to a hostess bar. The smell of cheap perfume and a faint odor of bathing bubbles is in the air. Out-of-tune sounds of a karaoke waft out to the street.

KENNY: **Jinsei benkyo no tame ni haitte miyo ze. Aitsura to wa mata ato de. Konbanwa. Ne chan.**

TARO:	Hold the Japanese, she's a **Japayuki**.
KENNY:	This place is full of **"jugun ian fu."**
MAMA-SAN:	**Yoyaku no nai okyakusan wa o kotowari shite orimasu. Chotto gaijin-sama dame desu.**
TARO:	**Hai, wakarimashita.**
KENNY:	**Gaijin sabetsu desu ka?**
YAKUZA:	**Nanka fu-tsugo ga arimashitaka?**
KENNY:	**Doushite gaikokujin hairenai? O mizu no sekai ni wa gaikokujin iru, desho?**
YAKUZA:	**Baka yaro, teme no shita koto ka!**
KENNY:	**Nan dayo nan dayo omae-wa?**
YAKUZA:	**Kono kusottare. Itaime-ni aitai no ka? Monku ga aru nara soto ni dero.**

Dialogue in English

KENNY:	Let's take a look to learn about the human condition. We'll meet Nigel and the gals at the disco. Good evening, sister.
TARO:	Hold the English, she's a **Japayuki**.
KENNY:	This place is full of "comfort women."
MAMA-SAN:	If you don't have a reservation, I'm afraid we can't seat you. *(to Taro)* Sorry, no foreigners.
TARO:	Yes, I understand.
KENNY:	Are you prejudiced against foreigners?
YAKUZA:	What seems to be the problem here?
KENNY:	How come you don't let foreigners in? Why, you've even got foreign girls working here!
YAKUZA:	Fool! It's none of your fuckin' business!
KENNY:	And who the fuck are you?
YAKUZA:	Shit-face, you want to feel pain, step outside.

Vocabulary

jinsei benkyo	the human condition
aitsura	those rats
Japayuki	a Southeast Asian hostess
jugun ian fu	"comfort women," involuntary sex slaves to Japan's Imperial Army, mostly recruited from neighboring Asian countries
gaijin sabetsu	prejudice against foreigners
fu-tsugo ga arimashitaka?	Something the matter?
o mizu	girls of the water trade, prostitutes, massage girls
baka yaro	stupid asshole
teme no shitta koto ka	none of your fuckin' business
nan dayo omae-wa	Who the fuck do you think you are?
kono kusottare	this asshole
itaime-ni	You want to feel some real pain?

Mama-san

The mama-san tries to make peace, but the yakuza starts pushing Kenny out.

MAMA-SAN: **Yamete, kenka ni natte omawari san no osewa ni naru no, iya yo.**

KENNY: If you touch me, you'll be sorry.

YAKUZA: Sorry? **Wakatara tsumami dasareru mae ni, tottoto dete ike!**

KENNY: **Chikusho!**

YAKUZA: **Zakennayo!**

Zakennayo!

Dialogue in English

MAMA-SAN: Stop it. If you keep on fighting, the cops will come, and that's bad news.

KENNY: If you touch me, you'll be sorry.

YAKUZA: Sorry? If you're sorry you better split before you get the heave-ho.

KENNY: You beast!

YAKUZA: Fuck off!

Time to Run

Kenny and Taro beat a quick exit without waiting for an answer.

TARO: **Abunai yo. Sakki no panchi wa yat-chan dayo. Mon-mon mitaka?**

KENNY: **Onigawara mitai na, gesu datta na.**

TARO: **Mite, gaijin ga seikan massaji ni haitte-iku! Baita ga suki mitai.**

KENNY: **Dekai guzu to zurui chibi, aitsura motenai kara, kane ni mono o iwasete.**

TARO: **Kusatta gaijin.**

KENNY: **Gaijin kadoka kankenai, kusatta ningen da.**

TARO: **Kono hen wa, tachinbo mo ooi shi, raritta yatsu bakari da na.**

KENNY: **Honto?**

TARO: **Chinpira, boso zoku, himo, yaku no bai nin, mekake.**

KENNY: **Mo chotto ochitsukeru tokoro ni iko.**

Dialogue in English

TARO: It's dangerous here. That guy with the Brillo hair was a gangster. Did you see his tattoos?

KENNY: He looked like a gargoyle. Ugly creep.

TARO: Oh, look, there's foreigners going into the sexual massage parlor. Looks like the idiot and short stuff going in for some whores.

KENNY: They're so hard up they have to buy women.

TARO: Those stinking foreigners.

KENNY: It's not because they're foreigners.

TARO: There's a lot of street hookers around here, not to mention the druggies.

KENNY: Really?

TARO: Punks, motorcycle gangs, pimps, drug dealers, and mistresses.

KENNY: Let's go to a nicer part of town.

Vocabulary

omawari	cop, police
iya yo	bad situation, undesirable course of events
tsumami dasareru mae ni	before you get the heave-ho
tottoto dete ike	Get the fuck out of here!
chikusho	beast; a standard but pungent insult, fighting words
panchi	punch perm; i.e., *yakuza* with trademark knotty hairstyle
yat-chan	*yakuza*
mon-mon	tattoo, *irezumi*
onigawara	gargoyle
gesu	ugly (man), low class
terebi ana-unsa	TV reporter, TV announcer

74

seikan massaji	sexually oriented massage parlors, hard-core
baita	whore, prostitute
dekai guzu	big idiot
zurui chibi	sneaky dwarf
kane ni mono o iwaseru	They use money to get it.
kusatta gaijin	stinking, rotten foreigners
kusatta ningen	rotten people

tachinbo	street hooker
raritta	undesirables, druggies
chinpira	punk, hoodlum
boso zoku	motorcycle gang
himo	pimp; from the Japanese for *string*, as in a man who keeps a lady on a string
yaku no bai nin	drug dealer
mekake	kept woman of a rich man
ochitsukeru tokoro	relaxed place, nicer part of town
iko	Let's go.

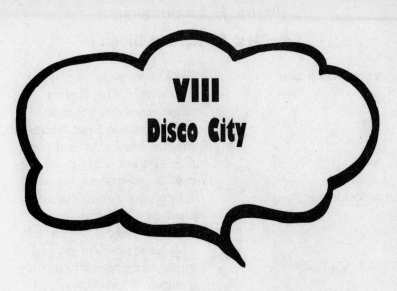

VIII
Disco City

Roppongi

Roppongi is the "designated" play spot for foreigners in Tokyo. Roppongi, written with three look-alike characters that together mean six trees, is located near a former U.S. military compound and not far from the U.S. Embassy and several big hotels. Foreigners are expected, even encouraged, to spend their money there. Other neighborhoods, such as Akasaka or Ginza or Kabuki-cho, have a more "Japanese" image. "Japanese" nightlife revolves around the sexual needs and fantasies of Japanese men; thus, these neighborhoods are neither attractive, enticing, nor recommended as places for foreigners going out for drinks.

Beauties, Sluts, and Bimbos

roppongi gyaru
the Roppongi girl, a playgirl, a Yellow cab. This slightly negative epithet suggests "fallen woman," not because she has lost her virginity or likes sex, but because she does it with foreigners.

iero kyabu
Yellow cab, a term coined by Japanese journalists to describe "easy" Japanese girls who let themselves get picked up by foreigners. Presumably inspired by the plethora of Yellow cabs on the streets of New York that pick up passengers without discrimination. Based on the obviously naive observation that New York cabs are "easy to pick up."

ko gyaru
Ko means little, and *gyaru* comes from the English word *girl*, but in this context it means playgirl; thus, a *ko gyaru* is a little playgirl, usually a high school student.

bodicon
If you see a pretty girl in a tight dress that fits her voluptuous body to a *t*, then you might be tempted to say *"bodicon."* Originally a fashion term, *bodicon* refers

to a "body-conscious" dresser, usually a disco queen or professional hostess.

para gyaru
a "paradise" girl, a variation on the *ike-ike* disco queen

kyapi kyapi gyaru
a combination of Japanese onomatopoeia and girl, meaning "happy happy girl," a spoiled, worry-free female creature, or what Americans might call a bimbo

charai
a little lower on the popularity list, perhaps akin to calling a woman an easy lay; originally from the Kansai dialect of west Japan

Saitama girls
(also *Chiba girls*) the overly dressed suburban girls who pretend to be urban sophisticates, but are usually real-life Cinderellas in princess garb under great pressure to catch the last pumpkin train home; sometimes called *dasai-tama*, or *chiba-ragi* (variations on the prefectural names) meaning, in short, dumb hicks. These would-be sophisticates are Tokyo's answer to "Jersey girls" or "Staten Island girls."

Japanese girls don't get mad, they get even. Here's how they refer to boys that are useful to them:

ashi kun	footman, good for a ride home
meshi kun	foodman, good for a free meal
neshi kun	sleepman, good for a lay
mitsugu kun	supplyman, good for favors in general
eigo kun	English lesson man, good for practicing English with
onna tarashi	playboy, lady-killer; the more accomplished members of this tribe aspire to be *hyaku nin giri* (man of a hundred conquests)

Bodicon Dancers

Nigel, Kenny, and Taro enter a crowded disco. Miniskirted girls are dancing on a high stage showing off their young, supple bodies.

KENNY: Yatta! Otachidai-gyaru no arashi da.
TARO: Bodicon, t-bakku mo, ima ichi dana.
NIGEL: O-utsukushi kata ooi desu ne.
KENNY: Miro, miro! Ano ko wa O-back mitai dazo!
TARO: Panchira dokoro ka, marumie tte kanji dana.
KENNY: Kaburi-tsuki made iko-yo.
NIGEL: Watashi wa koko de ii desu.
TARO: Ja, kabe no hana ni nattero.

Dialogue in English

KENNY: Oh wow, the stage is overflowing with go-go girls.

TARO: Tight dresses, thong-back panties, it does nothing for me.

NIGEL: There are so many beautiful young ladies here!

KENNY: Look, look! She's wearing panties with a hole in the back.

TARO: Yeah, check out those panties! I can see the whole world.

KENNY: Let's go up to the stage for a closer look.

NIGEL: I'll stay back here, if you don't mind.

TARO: Then you're a wallflower.

Vocabulary

otachidai-gyaru	the disco stage girls, go-go girls
bodicon	body-conscious fashion; tight, revealing dresses
imaichi	doesn't turn me on
O-back	panties with a hole in the back
panchira	panties showing
marumie	can see it all, revealing
kaburi-tsuki	stage front in a strip joint
kabe no hana ni natero	You'll turn into a wallflower.

Sugar Daddy

Nigel is wandering around alone on the dance floor.

NIGEL: **Watashi to issho ni odotte kudasai masenka?**

YUMI: **Dansu mo ii kedo, nanka nomanai?**

NIGEL: **Ja, watashi ga gochi so shimasu.**

YUMI: **Yappi. Kyo no meshi kun kore de kimari.**

82

Zakennayo!

RUMI: **Demo, mottainaiyo. Chotto buriko shite, kanezuru no mitsugu-kun sureba?**

YUMI: **Demo anta ki o tsuke na kya, gaijin wa te ga hayai shi, eizu mo kowai shi.**

Dialogue in English

NIGEL: Could I have the pleasure of the next dance?

YUMI: Dancing's fine, but I'm thirsty. What about a drink?

NIGEL: I see, let the drinks be on me, then.

YUMI: Goody. We've got our food and drinks man for this night.

RUMI: But, it's a shame. If you play it right, you could make him into a real young sugar daddy by being cute.

YUMI: You have to be careful with foreigners, they've got hands like an octopus, and you've heard the scare stories about AIDS.

Vocabulary

nanka nomanai	Shouldn't we be drinking?
gochi so shimasu	Thank you for the treat.
yappi	happy happy, hippity, hoppity
meshi kun	meal boy, a guy good for a free meal
motainaiyo	It's a waste.
buriko	cutie cutie
kanezuru	gold mine
mitsugu-kun	young sugar daddy, gift buyer
ki o tsuke na kya	You better watch out!
te ga hayai	hands are fast, an octopus

eizu   AIDS, a disease
                            unfortunately associated
                            with foreigners

Bottoms Up!

RUMI: **Kanpai!**

NIGEL: **Shitsurei shimashita. Watashi no namae wa Nigel desu. Kore wa watashi no meshi desu.**

YUMI: **Uso! Yada! Honto? NHK no hito? Sugoi jan?**

RUMI: **Watashi wa Rumi, kono ko wa Yumi. Yoropiku ne!**

KENNY: **Ki o tsukete, kare wa o-usotsuki, yarase no senmonka dayo.**

YUMI: **Shitteru hito?**

NIGEL: **Hai, kare wa watashi no tomodachi desu. Taro wa doko?**

KENNY: **Wakannai. Kanojo tachi, konbanwa, mabu dachi no Kenny desu. Oretachi wa dokushin-kizoku desu.**

NIGEL: **Kenny wa putaro desu.**

YUMI: **Yumi wa nodo ga kawai chatta.**

RUMI: **Rumi mo.**

KENNY: **Koko wa urusai kara, boku no shitteru gaijin ba ni iko yo.**

Dialogue in English

RUMI: Cheers!

NIGEL: Excuse me for not properly introducing myself. My name is Nigel. This is my card.

YUMI: No, no way. Are you for real? An employee of NHK? Isn't that something!

RUMI: I'm Rumi, she's Yumi. Happy to see you.

KENNY: Watch out, girls, he's a big liar, he works in the propaganda business.

YUMI: You know this guy?

NIGEL: Yes, he is my friend. Where is Taro?

KENNY: I don't know. Hey there, girls, Kenny's the name, and he's my best buddy. We're in the bachelor tribe.

NIGEL: Kenny is a bum.

YUMI: Yumi's throat is all dry.

RUMI: Me, too.

KENNY: It's too noisy here. Let's go to a **gaijin** bar.

Vocabulary

uso	you lie
yada	no way
honto?	Really?
sugoi jan?	Isn't that great?
yoropiku ne!	Oh, I'm so pitter-patter happy.
yarase	faking, trickery
mabu dachi	best friend
dokushin-kizoku	bachelor tribe
putaro	a lazy bum, on the dole, just hangs out

Zakennayo!

Yumi, Rumi using your name instead of the pronoun *I* is a bit on the cute side

kawai chata dried up; I'm thirsty.

gaijin ba *gaijin* bar, expatriate hangout

IX
Foreign Drinking Holes

Although Tokyo is dotted with interesting bars and clubs that anyone can go to, if you are a *gaijin* looking for other *gaijin* in a lively multicultural neighborhood full of nightlife offerings, Roppongi is the only game in town.

Gaijin Bar

Nigel, Kenny, Yumi, and Rumi visit a trendy bar crammed with foreigners of every description. Along the way the girls have a private chat about the boys.

YUMI: **Koitsu asobinin pokute, abuna-so.**
RUMI: **Nihongo pera pera dakara, Eigo-kun ni mo dekinai shi.**
YUMI: **Nihon ni iru gaijin-te, nanpa yarou bakka jan. Kotchi miteru.**
RUMI: **Kore nondara, zurakaro yo.**
YUMI: **Kyo wa kareshi no uchi ni otomari suru shi.**

Zakennayo!

The four of them enter the bar.

YUMI: Dai shokku, gaijin bakari!
RUMI: Takoku-sekigun tte kanji.
KENNY: Itaria go de kanpai-te nante iu ka shiteru?
YUMI: Yumi wakanai.
RUMI: Rumi mo wakanai.
KENNY: Kenny mo wakanai.
RUMI: Yada! nante iu no?
KENNY: Chu shite kuretara, oshiete ageru.
RUMI: Gaijin-te, sugu kisu shitagaru-n-dakara.
YUMI: Nihon no onna no ko-te sonnani kantan ni kisu shinai wayo.

Dialogue in English

YUMI: This character looks like a playboy. He's dangerous.
RUMI: His Japanese is good. I don't think we can cop any English off him.
YUMI: The foreigners who live in Japan are really into picking up girls.
RUMI: Let's split after the next drink.
YUMI: Tonight I'm going to crash with my old man.

YUMI: How shocking, it's all foreigners!
RUMI: It looks like the multinational forces.
KENNY: Does anyone here know how to say "cheers" in Italian?
YUMI: Yumi doesn't know.
RUMI: Rumi doesn't know either.
KENNY: Kenny doesn't know.
RUMI: What do you mean?

89

KENNY: I'll tell you if you give me a kiss.
RUMI: You foreigners, you just kiss so easily.
YUMI: We Japanese girls aren't as easy as you think when it comes to kissing.

Vocabulary

koitsu	this little rat
asobinin pokute	looks like a player, playboy, playgirl
abuna-so	looks dangerous
nanpa yarou bakka jan	always on the make
kotchi miteru	He is looking at me.
zurakaro	to escape, take the money and run
kareshi	my him, boyfriend
otomari suru	spend the night
dai shokku	How shocking!
takoku-sekigun tte kanji	It just feels so full of multinational troops.
yada	no way
chu	kiss
sugu kisu shitagaru	want to kiss right away
kantan	simple, easy (as in "easy lay")
wayo	feminine verb ending

Bimbo Heaven

Nigel, ever the gentleman, goes to the crowded bar to buy yet another round of drinks.

YUMI: Nigel-te, kanojo iru no?

KENNY: Nigel ga ki-ni-itta? Migi te ga koi-bito. Kimitachi boifurendo inai no?

YUMI and RUMI: Hoshi kedo, inai no.
KENNY: Boku ni mo inai.
NIGEL: Osake ga kimashita.
KENNY: Kanpai! Chin-chin!
YUMI: Ge-ge? Etchi gaijin shinjiraenai.
KENNY: Etchi janai yo. Chin-chin wa
                   Itaria-go de kampai no koto. Etchi
                   wa sotchi.
NIGEL: Chotto shitsurei shimasu, senmenjo
                   ni ittekimasu.

Dialogue in English

YUMI: Does Nigel have a girlfriend?
KENNY: Why are you interested? His only
                   girlfriend is his right hand. And you
                   two, any boyfriends?
YUMI and RUMI: I want a boyfriend, but I haven't found
                   one yet.
NIGEL: Drinks have arrived.
KENNY: Let's drink to that, "chin-chin."
YUMI: Disgusting. How can you say that, you
                   dirty-minded foreigner?
KENNY: That's not dirty. "Chin-chin" is how
                   you say "cheers" in Italian. You're the
                   one with a dirty mind.
NIGEL: Excuse me, gentleman and ladies. I
                   must go to the powder room.

Curfew Time

The girls give each other a knowing glance.

YUMI: Kenny wa ikanakute daijobu?

KENNY: Nigel to tsureshon nanka shitakunai yo. Tokoro de, kimi no denwa bango wa?

YUMI: Mama mo Papa mo Eigo dekinai kara Kenny ga kakete kitara bikkuri shi-chau.

KENNY: Ja, kore wa boku no denwa bango. Poketto-beru desu kara, itsu demo denwa shite.

NIGEL: Shitsurei shimashita.

RUMI: Soro-soro kaerimasu. Mo sugu mongen nano.

YUMI: Watashi mo mongen nanno. Beron-beron ja nai kedo yotta mitai. Gochisosama.

NIGEL: Do itashimashite.

YUMI and RUMI: Bai-bai!

KENNY: Nigel, we're wasting our time on these **kyapi-kyapi** gals from the **potato-sen.** Let's find the others.

Dialogue in English

YUMI: Kenny, don't you have to go too?

KENNY: What do you think, I want to cross-piss with Nigel in the toilet? While you're still here, what's your telephone number?

YUMI: Mama and Papa can't speak English.

	They will be shocked to get a phone call from a foreigner.
KENNY:	Well, here's my number, just call my beeper.
NIGEL:	I'm back again.
RUMI:	We have to go now. It's almost curfew time.
YUMI:	Me too. We're not as plastered as you think. Thanks for the treat!
NIGEL:	Don't mention it, the pleasure's mine.
YUMI and RUMI:	Good-bye.
KENNY:	Nigel, we're wasting our time on these bimbos from the sticks. Let's find the others.

Vocabulary

kanojo	girlfriend
ki-ni-itta?	Are you interested?
boifurendo	boyfriend, lover
migi te ga koibito	his only lover is his right hand; he beats the meat
chin-chin	penis, dick
ge-ge?	What? Huh?
etchi wa sotchi	You're the one who is perverted.
senmenjo	wash-face place; euphemism for toilet
ikanakute daijobu?	Is it okay not to go?
tsureshon	cross-pissing; two guys take a slash together
bikkuri shi-chau	I am shocked.
poketto-beru	Pocket Bell, a telephone pager
soro-soro	time to leave; It's getting late.

94

mongen	curfew
beronberon	plastered, drunk
gochisosama	Thanks for treating me.
bai-bai	bye-bye, usually said with a loud, childish whine
kyapi-kyapi	bimbo, Japanese version of L.A. "Valley Girls"
potato-sen	"potato line" (refers to a rural train line in Saitama)

X
After Hours

Roppongi can be very expensive, especially if you drink. All trains stop running shortly after midnight, usually just at the time that things are getting interesting. But by three or four in the morning there is almost no place to go. Taxi prices are astronomical, so you might find yourself nursing a coffee in a greasy spoon until the first train of the morning. All-night fast-food restaurants are the most interesting places in town starting at four a.m.

Donut Shop

Taro is eating a cinnamon donut and slurping his coffee. Meanwhile, in the ladies' room . . .

SHARON: **Yadda. Do shiyo. Kyu ni okyaku-san ga kita-mitai.**
KEIKO: **Seiri na no? Napukin aru wa yo.**
SHARON: **Tampon no hoga ii.**
KEIKO: **Eh? Tampon-te asoko ni ireru toki itakunai?**

SHARON: **Zenzen. Demo Nigel no uchi ni tomaru tsumori datta no ni.**

KEIKO: **Honto ni? So iu naka datta no?**

SHARON: **Baka iwanai de yo. Tada no keep-kun yo.**

KEIKO: **Sore ja, Taro no koto wa dou na no? Ganchu ni nai no?**

SHARON: **So ja nai no. Kare ni wa karuku mirareta-kunai no.**

KEIKO: **Sonna koto ittetara, asoko ni kumo no su ga haru wa yo.**

Dialogue in English

SHARON: Oh no! What should I do? I think my period's come.

KEIKO: That time of month? I have some Kotex.

SHARON: I like to use tampons.

KEIKO: Really? But doesn't it hurt when you put it in?

SHARON: Not at all, but I'm planning to spend the night at Nigel's.

KEIKO: Really? You and him are hitting it off?

SHARON: Don't be ridiculous, he's just a useful friend.

KEIKO: Tell me, what's going on with Taro? Can't you see it?

SHARON: It's not that, but I don't want him to take me for an easy lay.

KEIKO: With that attitude you'll find your pussy in cobwebs.

Vocabulary

okyaku-san ga kita-mitai	looks like my period's here (literally, My guest has arrived.)
seiri	menstruation
napukin	Kotex, sanitary napkin
asoko ni ireru	put it in there
so iu naka	not in that sense
baka iwanai de yo	Don't be stupid!
keep-kun	a good useful male companion
ganchu ni nai	Aren't you interested in him?
karuku miraretakunai no	I don't want to be taken for an easy lay.
kumo no su ga haru	pussy is covered up with cobwebs; needs a good fuck

Chance Encounter

Taro spots Nigel and Kenny walking the streets and waves them into the donut shop.

TARO: Hey, **gaijinzu.**
SHARON: Where'd you go? We've been waiting in this
              joint forever!

KENNY: Nigel no nanpa ni tsukiattetan da.
NIGEL: Sonna koto gozaimasen.

Yumi and Rumi enter the donut shop with their boyfriends.

TARO: Miro. Nigel makka dazo. Kanojo tachi doshita
            no?
NIGEL: Hako iri musume dakara, mongen ga aru.
KENNY: Mite, mite! Nigel no "koibito" no Yumi to
            Rumi ga kita! Otoko mo issho da.
NIGEL: Yumi-san, Rumi-san mata oai shimashita ne.

*Yumi and Rumi don't see Nigel and Kenny until it is too late,
so they ignore them.*

NIGEL: Yumi-san . . . Rumi?
TARO: Nigel no "ojosama" no kare wa chinpira
            mitai.
KEIKO: Nigel-chan ga kawai-so ja nai?
KENNY: Kenny mo kawai-so. Kon ya wa hitori-ne da.
TARO: Nigel no uchi ni ippaku sasete-kurerun
            daro?
NIGEL: Mina-san de dozo. Go enryo naku.
KEIKO: Arigato, demo kyo wa kaeru.
KENNY: Okutte-kuyo.
TARO: Kenny okuri-okami ni naru na yo.
SHARON: Taro wa okami ni wa naranai no?
TARO: Boku wa feminisuto desu.

Dialogue in English

TARO: Hey, two gaijin!
SHARON: Where did you go? We've been waiting in this
            joint forever!

KENNY:	Nigel was picking up girls inside.
NIGEL:	It wasn't as he says.
TARO:	Look! Nigel is blushing! Where're your girls now?
NIGEL:	They are the conservative types. They had to go home before curfew.
KENNY:	Hey, guys! Check it out. Nigel's girls Yumi and Rumi are over there. And look, they're with some guys.
NIGEL:	Yumi, Rumi, hi! We meet again.
NIGEL:	Yumi . . . Rumi . . .
TARO:	It looks like his "good" girls are going out with street hoods.
KEIKO:	Poor little Nigel.
KENNY:	Poor me, too. It looks like I'll be sleeping alone again.
TARO:	Nigel, would it be okay if I crashed at your house tonight?
NIGEL:	Everyone is welcome to stay at my place. Don't stand on ceremony.
KEIKO:	Thanks, but tonight I must go home.
KENNY:	I'll see you home.
TARO:	Watch out. Kenny will not be satisfied to stop at the door.
SHARON:	And Taro, you wouldn't be tempted to do the same?
TARO:	No, because I'm a gentleman.

Vocabulary

ojosama	preppy girl, aristocratic young lady
chinpira	a street punk, young hood

gaijinzu	two or more *gaijin*
tsukiattetan da	the one's he befriended
makka	blush, turn dark red
hako iri musume	good old-fashioned girl
hitori-ne	sleep all alone
ippaku	crash for the night
okutte-kuyo	I'll see you home.
okuri-okami	a see-you-home wolf, scheming man
feminisuto	gentleman (as in the type who opens doors for ladies); does not mean feminist in American sense

XI
Romance
and Lowlife

Yoyogi Park is Tokyo's answer to New York's Central Park. The circular park, with American-style landscaping, is wedged in between the national icons of Meiji Shrine, Olympic Pool, and NHK TV station, but that doesn't mean funky things don't happen there. High school kids having sex in the bushes, rock singers getting stoned, yakuza running protection rackets, pickpockets looking for marks, homeless bums taking naps, and, more recently, unemployed Iranians giving one another haircuts are among the more predictable sights. As Tokyo matures, taking a walk in the park is turning into something of an adventure.

For starters, it's not unusual to find homeless drifters bathing in the restrooms. On the other hand, despite the fact that public toilets can be found in every corner of Tokyo, Japanese men, including the homeless, seem to prefer the outdoor piss. Maybe that's because city parks sport doorless, open-air public toilets, which don't offer much more privacy than taking a leak outside anyway.

Generally speaking, Japanese have a more matter-of-fact attitude about bodily functions, and this is reflected in the rich variety of perfectly acceptable ways to say shit and ass, with the result that both terms lack the punch they have in English.

furosha	floating vagrant, homeless
regee no ojisan	Uncle Reggae, bum with dirty matted hair
regei	homeless
nozoki	Peeping Tom
chikan	pervert, molester
panti dorobo	panty thief (usually grabs panties off clothesline)
pin hane	protection money, collected by Yakuza from vendors around park
yatai	stands selling food and drink, usually without legal title to the land they use
iran jin	Iranian workers, often congregating in parks on Sundays
tekiya	mob-related vendors who work the food stands
koshubenjo	public toilet
otearai	washroom
senmenjo	restroom
keshoshitsu	powder room
unko	shit
unchi	shit
unching style	squatting, as in taking a shit
kuso	shit
noguso	field shit, squatting position
shonben	piss
tachi shon	take a leak (standing)
oshikko	urination

shishi take a pee (female)
man shon cunt shower (a play on words that sounds like mansion)

Philip J. Cunningham

A Walk in the Park

Kenny and Keiko take a moonlit stroll through Yoyogi Park, but she spurns his advances.

KENNY: Konya wa tanoshikatta, yoake no kohi o issho ni nomitai.

KEIKO: Ya yo. Nigel nara sonna koto wa iwanai wa.

KENNY: Etchi shitai.

KEIKO: Nigel wa riso no otoko yo.

KENNY: Horetano?

KEIKO: Nigel wa sanko de, hansamu de, ogyogi mo ii.

KENNY: Ja nande ore to issho ni irunda?

KEIKO: Datte ishibe kinkichi de tsumaranain damon.

KENNY: Mite, regee no ojisan tachishon shiteru.

KEIKO: Anbiribaboo! Koshu benjo aru ja nai?

KENNY: Keiko no koto?

KEIKO: Gehin ne.

Dialogue in English

KENNY: I had a good time tonight. Let's have coffee together in the morning.

KEIKO: Uh-uh. Nigel would never say a thing like that.

KENNY: I want to do it with you.

KEIKO: Nigel is such an ideal type.

KENNY: Do you have the hots for him?

KEIKO: Nigel is tall, rich, and brainy. He's handsome and has good manners.

KENNY: So, what are you doing with me?

KEIKO: It's not easy being with Mr. Perfect.

KENNY: Oh, look! That homeless man is taking a piss!

KEIKO: That's unbelievable! What's wrong with the public toilet?

KENNY: Are you one?
KEIKO: Disgusting.

Vocabulary

yoake no kohi issho ni shitai	Let's have morning coffee; actually means "Let's spend the night together."
ya yo	no sirree
etchi shitai	I want to have sex.
horetano	to have the hots for
sanko	the three heights: tall stature, high education, high salary
hansamu	(from English) handsome
sanryo	the three goods: good face, good personality, good family
gyogi ga ii	good manners
datte ishibe kinkichi	but he's so straight and uptight
rege no ojisan	Uncle Reggae, a homeless man with matted hair
tachishon shiteru	take a piss, take a whiz
anbiribaboo!	from *unbelievable*, which is unbelievably hard to pronounce in Japanese
koshu benjo	public toilet
Keiko no koto?	implication that Keiko is a *koshu benjo* (a woman who "does" anything)
gehin	low-class, vulgar, uncouth

Getting Frisky

Kenny gooses Keiko, to her great surprise.

KENNY: Chikan ni atta koto aru?
KEIKO: Yada! Mo kaeranakucha.
KENNY: Suman, doshite Keiko wa sugu ni heso o mageru?
KEIKO: Shuden dechatta. Do shiyo?
KENNY: Asa made tsukiao yo.
KEIKO: Ja takushi de kaeru kara, issho ni hirotte?
KENNY: Sore nara, koko de. Baibi.
KEIKO: Matte yo. Oite ikanai de.
KENNY: Dasai disuko de, suge ase kaita shi, tabako kusai kara, shawa abitai.
KEIKO: Kenny no uchi mo tooi ja nai?
KENNY: Ore wa, teruho no waribiki ken motteru kara, issho ni ikouka?
KEIKO: Watashi, nomisugichatta mitai.
KENNY: Gero hakunayo!
KEIKO: Daijobu, demo koko ni itemo shoganai shi.
KENNY: Ja, sukoshi yasunde iko yo.

Dialogue in English

KENNY: Have you ever met a pervert?
KEIKO: Stop it. I'm going home now.
KENNY: So sorry, Charlie. Why are you suddenly all bent out of shape?
KEIKO: The last train is gone. What can I do?
KENNY: Let's hang out till morning.
KEIKO: Do you want to help me find a taxi?
KENNY: If that's your attitude, let's split right here. Bye!
KEIKO: Wait! Don't go . . .

Zakennayo!

KENNY: I'm all sweated up and smoky from that stupid disco. I have to take a shower.

KEIKO: Isn't your place far from here?

KENNY: I've got some discount coupons for a nearby hotel. Want to go with me?

KEIKO: I feel a bit drunk.

KENNY: Just don't puke on me!

KEIKO: I'm okay, but I want to get out of here.

KENNY: Okay, let's go for a little rest.

Vocabulary

chikan	pervert, subway molester
yada! mo kaeranakucha	That does it! I've got to go home.
suman	so sorry (from *sumimasen*)
sugu heso o mageru	belly button is twisted, bent out of shape
shuden dechatta	The last train of the night is gone (an excuse to spend the night together).
tsukiao	Let's be together.
hirotte	Grab a cab.
Ja, koko de. Baibi.	Let's say good-bye here (a childish variation of the already childish "bye-bye").
oite ikanai de	Don't leave me behind.
dasai disuko	that stupid disco
suge ase kaita shi	all sweated up
tabako kusai	stinks of cigarette smoke
teruho no waribiki ken	discount coupons for the hotel
nomisugichatta	drunk, drank too much
gero hakunayo	Just don't puke on me.

shoganai   I can't take it anymore.
ja, sukoshi yasunde iko yo Let's go for a little rest;
                        sounds innocent, but actually
                        means "Let's go to a love
                        hotel."

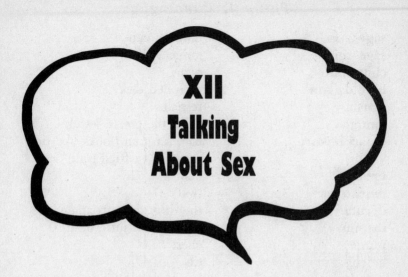

XII
Talking About Sex

Love hotel is one of those unforgettable Japanese-English words with sexual connotations, right up there with *skinship* and *soaplands*. Here's some vocabulary that might come in handy in a love hotel, called *rabu ho* for short. What better time to brush up on the names of body parts in Japanese?

Then again, there comes a certain point in the evening where you stop talking and let your bodies communicate. You probably won't have to say these words, unless you are playing "Simon says" in bed, but you will want to know them just in case. One respectable way to break the ice when talking about places on the body where the sun doesn't shine is to talk about movies. Mention that you like the works of director Juzo Itami, especially the film *Ageman*. But what does the title mean? *Age man* means lucky cunt, and although everyone knows what it means, it won't be easy to get a proper explanation. By the way, *age chin* is the male equivalent, which means lucky dick. Good luck.

age man	lucky cunt
age chin	lucky dick

sage man	unlucky cunt
sage chin	unlucky dick
chin-chin	penis
hine daikon	shriveled dick
kyusho	testicles
kintama	balls, the crown jewels
oinari bukuro	bag, scrotum (looks like rice wrapped in fried tofu)
omanko	cunt
omeko	twat
deruta	the dirty delta, triangle
mammae	clitoris (the little bean)
mune	chest
chichi	tits
oppai	breasts
reizunpai	raisin tits, flat as a raisin pie (*pai* is slang for tit)
koshi	hips, often confused with ass in polite society
shiri ga aoi	"blue ass," young, blue spot (Mongolian birthmark)
shiri ga omoi	"heavy ass," slow, lazy
shiri ga karui	"light ass," an easy lay
shiri ni hi ga tsuku	"a fire under your butt," get moving
shiri o nuguu	"wipe ass," clean up after someone
shipetta	buns, ass
ketsu no ana	asshole
kikuza	fancy way to say asshole (literally, chrysanthemum)
fakku	fuck
sekkusu	sounds like sex, but meaning restricted to intercourse
beddoin	have sex in bed

skinship	the relationship of two naked bodies
irete kudasai	insert please, put it in, do me, fuck me
manko yaro	want to screw some pussy
auto-sekkusu	masturbation
senzuri	beat the meat
manzuri	twat massage
paizuri	rub dick in between breasts, give a pearl necklace
seishi	spermatozoa
iku	come
karupisu	loving spoonful
fera	fellatio
ainame	mutual licking
sikkusu nain	mutual oral sex, 69
hitori etchi	self-stimulation

Tryst at Maruyama-cho

Kenny and Keiko walk hand in hand from Yoyogi Park to a nearby love hotel in Shibuya's Maruyama-cho. They rent a room for the night and sit down on the king-size bed. There is an awkward moment of silence.

KENNY: **Eibui miru?**
KEIKO: **Oyu irete kuru.**
KENNY: **Chotto kite miro yo.**
KEIKO: **Yada, nani!**
KENNY: **Shiranai no? Bata-ken dayo!**
KEIKO: **Nande Kenny wa abunai seikatsu yamerarenai no?**
KENNY: **Abunakuneyo, kondo-san tsukatteru mon.**

KEIKO: **Katte ni shite. Watashi wa o furo ni haitte, saki ni yasumimasu.**

KENNY: **Dozo, ore wa eibui no tsuzuki o miru yo.**

Dialogue in English

KENNY: Hey, wanna watch a porno video?
KEIKO: I'm going to prepare the bath.
KENNY: Come, check this out!
KEIKO: Ugh! What's that?
KENNY: You don't know? That's "butter dog."

KEIKO: Kenny, why don't you give up your dangerous lifestyle?

KENNY: It's not dangerous. I always wear a cap.

KEIKO: Well, entertain yourself. I'm going to take a bath and then I'm going straight to bed.

KENNY: Be my guest. I want to watch this for a while.

Vocabulary

eibui	porno films (from *AV*)
miro yo	Check it out! Look!
yada, nani!	Ugh! What's that?
bata-ken	"butter dog": a porno scene where a woman's body is smeared with butter that is licked off by a dog
abunai seikatsu	dangerous lifestyle, sex-oriented lifestyle
abunakuneyo	It's not dangerous.
kondo-san	I'll wear Mr. Condom. (Kondo is a common last name.)
katte ni shite	Entertain yourself.

Getting Ready for Bed

Keiko comes out of the bath wearing nothing but a towel. Her hair is dripping wet, her cheeks glowing red.

KEIKO: **Ah, sappari shita.**

KENNY: **Keiko wa suppin mo kirei dane.**

KEIKO: **Yoku iwareru wa.**

KENNY: **Beddo dozo, ore wa yuka de ii yo.**

KEIKO: Ii otoko dane.
KENNY: Ja shawa shite koyotto.

Keiko gets dressed again before hopping into bed.

KEIKO: **Nani mo shinai nara, tonari ni nete mo ii wayo.**
KENNY: **Zannen, Kenny wa age chin nano ni.**
KEIKO: **Kenny, koibito inaino?**
KENNY: **So dana. Keiko no hatsu etchi wa?**
KEIKO: **Shotaiken? Hatachi. Kenny wa?**
KENNY: **Ore mada do-tei desu. Te-tori, ashi-tori oshiete kureyo.**
KEIKO: **Oyasumi nasai.**
KENNY: **Gaki mitai dakedo, te dake tsunai de, nete ii?**
KEIKO: **Sawaranai de hoshi no.**
KENNY: **Ja, te igai oppai to oshiri nara do?**
KEIKO: **Kenny honto ni kodomo mitai. Ii kagen ni shiteyo.**

Dialogue in English

KEIKO: Oh, that was refreshing!
KENNY: You know, you look good even without makeup.
KEIKO: That's what they all say.
KENNY: You can have the bed to yourself, I'll take the floor.
KEIKO: That's a good boy.
KENNY: Now it's time for my shower.

KEIKO: If you don't fool around, you can sleep next to me.
KENNY: That's too bad, I'm a lucky dick, you know.
KEIKO: Kenny, don't you have a girlfriend?

Zakennayo!

KENNY: That's a good question. Keiko, when was the first time you got laid?
KEIKO: My first sexual experience? I was twenty. And you?
KENNY: I'm still a virgin. Could you teach me the ropes?
KEIKO: Good night, Kenny.
KENNY: I don't want to be a pest, but do you think I could at least hold your hand?
KEIKO: I'd rather you keep your hands to yourself.
KENNY: Forget about holding hands, how about if I just fondle your tits and ass?
KEIKO: You're so immature! You had better behave yourself.

Vocabulary

ah, sappari shita	Ah, that was refreshing!
suppin	clean-faced, without makeup
yoku iwareru	That's what they all say, it's often said to me.
beddo dozo, ore wa yuka de ii yo	You take the bed, I'll manage on the floor. (Kenny is making a not-so-subtle bid for sympathy.)
ja shawa shite koyotto	I'm going to take my shower, that's what I'll do.
nani mo shinai	do nothing, i.e., no sex
age chin	lucky dick
so dana	Well, how can I put it? (an evasive answer if there ever was one)
hatsu etchi wa?	When did you first get laid?
shotaiken	first sexual experience

dou-tei	male virgin
te-tori, ashi-tori oshiete kureyo	Teach me the way of arms and legs; show me the ropes.
te dake tsunai de	Can I hold your hand?
sawaranai de hoshi no	I'd prefer if you didn't fondle me.
oppai to oshiri nara dou	How about just tits and ass?
ii kagen ni shiteyo	Be a good boy.

Sleepless in Tokyo

Kenny is tossing and turning in frustration.

KEIKO: **Neteta. Kenny wa nemurenai no?**

KENNY: **Asa dachi mitai noka? Ii onna no tonari de gugu netanjaa manuke daro.**

KEIKO: **Ji-pan nuide ii? Kenny ureshii, desho?**

KENNY: **Nugasete yaruyo. Ah, gomenasai, pan-tsu mo nugeta. Nanda yo omae. Nureteru ja nai ka. Ore no yume mita no ka?**

KEIKO: **Denki o keshite.**

KENNY: **Kimi no karada ga mitai.**

KEIKO: **Mune ga chisai kara hazukashii wa.**

KENNY: **Ketsu no ana mo chisai? Wa ha ha, jodan dayo. Tokoro de donna hana ga suki? Kikuza suki?**

KEIKO: **Kikuza te nani?**

KENNY: **Nandemo nai.**

Kenny starts to explore the cracks and crevices of Keiko's body.

KENNY: **Suponpon mo kirei da. Mochi hada ga suki. Inmo mo kawaii.**

KEIKO: **Itsu no mani hadaka ni nata no?**

Zakennayo!

Kenny pulls Keiko's naked, quivering body on top of his ...

KEIKO: **Kimochi ga ii wa.**
KENNY: **Ii nioi, oishiikedo chotto shoppai, kofun suru?**
KEIKO: **Naka ni kite.**
KENNY: **Aa! Shippai! maku toreta.**
KEIKO: **Iki so!**

Dialogue in English

KEIKO: I must have fallen asleep. Are you still awake?
KENNY: Looks like I have some company. It's a waste to sleep next to a beautiful woman.
KEIKO: May I take off my jeans? You're happy, aren't you?
KENNY: Let me take 'em off for you. Ah, sorry about that, looks like your panties have come off as well. Hey you, you're as wet as the ocean. You must have been dreaming about me.
KEIKO: Turn out the light.
KENNY: But I want to see your body.
KEIKO: My bust is small, I feel shy.
KENNY: Is your asshole small as well? Ha ha, I'm only joking. While we're on the topic, what kind of flowers do you like? How about chrysanthemum?
KEIKO: Chrysanthemum, what are you ...
KENNY: Never mind.

KENNY: You are also pretty with your clothes off. I like your soft, creamy skin. And look at these little pubic hairs.
KEIKO: Hey, who told you to take your clothes off?

KEIKO: That feels good.
KENNY: You smell good, you taste good, too, but a little
           salty. Getting excited?
KEIKO: Come inside of me.
KENNY: Shit, the condom popped off.
KEIKO: I'm coming!

Vocabulary

nemurenai?	Can't sleep?
asa dachi	"morning glory"; penile erection after waking up
gugu netanjaa manuke	foolish to sleep, no z's worth catching
ji-pan nuide ii?	Do you mind if I take off my jeans? (Kenny is a little slow; most Japanese girls wait to be undressed.)
nugasete yaruyo	I'll take 'em off for you.
aa! pan-tsu mo nugeta	Oops, your panties came off as well.
nureteru ja nai	Aren't you wet? (as in vaginal secretions, pussy juice)
mune ga chisai	My breasts are small; a standard and totally unnecessary apology
ketsu no ana mo chisai	Your asshole is also very small. This is a little pun based on a very standard way of saying to be stingy or cheap.
wa ha ha, jodan dayo	Ha, I'm only joking!
kikuza	literally, chrysanthemum; about the nicest way to say asshole

Zakennayo!

supponpon	stark naked, bare-assed
mochi hada	skin like *mochi*, a smooth, chewy sweet made from sticky rice
inmo	bush, pubic hair
hadaka	naked
ii nioi	You smell good.
oishiikedo, chotto shoppai	tastes good but a little salty
kofun suru?	Are you sexually aroused?
naka ni kite	Enter me, come inside.
maku ga toreta	The condom slipped off.
iki sou	Looks like I'm gonna come.

Coming Soon!

Keiko's moans and groans are now louder than the music.

KENNY: Shizuka ni shinasai!
KEIKO: Iku, iku! Irete!
KENNY: Senaka ni tsume o tateruna, itai yo!
KEIKO: Sugoi kanjiru, motto fukaku irete.
KENNY: Mada iretenai yo.

Kenny wa chitsu gai shasei shita.

KENNY: Gomen, ganmen shawa ni natchatta.
KEIKO: Hetakuso! Tisshu de karupisu fuite yo.
KENNY: Kashikomarimashita. Eh? Soko no kisumaaku wa dare no da?
KEIKO: Mochiron koibito no Nigel yo.

Dialogue in English

KENNY: Please keep quiet!
KEIKO: Ooh, ah, ooh, ah. Put it in!
KENNY: Ouch, you're clawing up my back!
KEIKO: That's so good, can you come in deeper?
KENNY: I'm not in yet!

Kenny has a seminal discharge.

KENNY: Oops! Did I give you a pearl necklace?
KEIKO: You clumsy fool, clean up the mess you made with a tissue.
KENNY: Yes ma'am. Hey, who gave you those hickeys?
KEIKO: My boyfriend Nigel, who else?

Zakennayo!

Vocabulary

iku iku	ooh, aah, "I'm coming!!!"
irete!	Put it in!
tsume o tateru	to claw someone, dig the nails in
sugoi kanjiru	that feels great
motto fukaku irete	deeper, deeper
mada iretenai yo	I'm not in yet.
Kenny wa chitsu gai shasei shita	Kenny has a seminal discharge.
ganmen shawa ni natchatta	looks like you got squirt in the face
Tisshu	tissue, Kleenex
hetakuso!	unskillful; That's the best you can do?
karupisu	Calpis, a white-colored soft drink, supposedly looks like come
fuite yo!	Wipe up!
kashikomarimashita	Yes ma'am, understood.
kisumaaku	hickeys, kiss marks
mochiron	Of course, who else would it be?

That's all for now, folks! *Sayonara* and good night.